More Praise for *It's Not Love Till Someone Loses an Eye*

The poems in *It's Not Love Till Someone Loses an Eye* balance on the edge of a chisel, where the beloved presents you with "a block of marble." Clay Ventre creates a remarkable place where lovers are gifted with a "cello/crawling with golden termites" and "a saxophone tarnished/with your suspicion." This may be the most accurate description of romance, of that "vast and empty space," where one meets the person "who would die for you/or melt cheese for you."

— Jennifer Martelli, author of *The Queen of Queens*

These poems let you eavesdrop on an intense lovers' dialogue at the table next to you, a dialogue completely unpredictable, comic and profound. They will refresh your views of love, and of poetry, and will make you leave the restaurant full of wonder. You should put down your fork and listen.

— J.D. Scrimgeour, author of *Banana Bread*

IT'S NOT LOVE TILL
SOMEONE LOSES AN EYE

CLAY VENTRE

Nixes Mate Books
Allston, Massachusetts

Copyright © 2023 Clay Ventre

Book design by d'Entremont

Cover photograph used with permission.

All rights reserved. This book or any portion thereof may not be reproduced or used in any manner whatsoever without the express written permission of the publisher except for the use of brief quotations in a book review or scholarly journal.

ISBN 978-1-949279-47-4

Nixes Mate Books
POBox 1179
Allston, MA 02134
nixesmate.pub

Every authentically loved being is a kind of god.

– Guy de Maupassant

CONTENTS

PROLOGUE

The Ungulate   3

IT'S NOT LOVE TILL SOMEONE LOSES AN EYE

How Best in Bronze to Show Your Feelings for Her   9
It's Bound to be Complicated   11
Soiree   13
Here   15
The Great Jiu Jitsu Move of Being   17
The Concert   18
Die a Little More   19
Hammers   20
Infinity War   21
The Art of Thinking on Earth at 3:13 AM   23
The Impossibility of Some Situations   24
Waking to the Sound of Cracking   26
How to Love a Ghost   27
Boredom Wasted on the Bored   28

It's Not Love Till Someone Loses an Eye	30
Breakfast all Day	31
Regnum Defende	33
Of a Feather	35
I Dreamed You Dammit	37
The Arrivalist	39
The Problems Show	40
Metamorphosis	42
Sleep	44
When Science Took Over or How to Believe a Queen When She Says "I Love You"	46
On a Self-Driving Couch to Somewhere	47

EPILOGUE

The Godless Night Kitchen (remodeled)	49

IT'S NOT LOVE TILL SOMEONE LOSES AN EYE

PROLOGUE

THE UNGULATE

I.

A stairway is not a tunnel
(per se) she said
and he said
yours are not the guts
that will grease the tracks
of any war machine
¡of mine

so satisfied and smiling they
– with a claxonmouthed
clown as sherpa –
clacked-off in their steel
rhinoceroses
to the zoo
to battle with the keepers
to keep
the snow leopard cubs from growing up and out
of what they are
and into the world

II.

Ray-guns and diners
are the same thing
(per se) he said
and she said
you'd not be the one I'd humiliate
in a stadium filled with
idiot archetypes

and so no words
like wasps between them
and where once they
knee-deep in cranberries
now is a choice of excavation
every shovelful is music
or money
or sometimes neither
but never both
Nowhere was a country
and Nothing a name
worth penning

III.

Her face –
– he voyaged for it

IV.

She explained the
movement of her feet
as "walking"
and the space she moved
through as
"/ˈTHerəpē/"

– he adjusted his understanding
of her to include the word
"exclusive"
and built a single-entry
encyclopedia for her to inhabit
she took him up on it
invited him in
and he stayed

V.

All outside
was Oslo and snow
(per se)
inside was all a giraffe
gentle and dying

I'd kill this thing for you
she said

I'd kill this thing for *you*
he said

and so they were warm
in the company of that lonely
– and increasingly nervous
animal

VI.

One thousand years
passed

VII.

A story is not
a tunnel (per se)
we say

theirs are not the clothes
we emerge in
– mottled furs
   from a dead innocent

one reluctant
to let the other's eyes
do all the seeing now

the other
reluctantly/tonguelessly
cedes all the talking now

¡What a pair!
(per se) we say
¿see?
winter is over

IT'S NOT LOVE TILL

SOMEONE LOSES AN EYE

HOW BEST IN BRONZE TO SHOW YOUR FEELINGS FOR HER

1.

Organize words into
tiny armies to invade
the shores of her
consciousness

2.

Hold your head
in your hands and
roll it up some
Sisyphean hill
named – Here is Where
the Hopeless Sigh

3.

Sigh

4.

Carve an immovable
statue of her

5.

Get used to it until
she shows up
carrying her
love
and a jackhammer

IT'S BOUND TO BE COMPLICATED

1.

Like how a guy named
Olaf gently shows you
the secret to decoding
runes before he runs you
through with a giant
rune-engraved sword
or
the cards you'll spend
a lifetime learning so
you can beat that certain
someone at their own
game – then when you
finally sit across
from her to play
she wins by default
because you just die
because the true meaning
of spending a lifetime
learning anything means
that your life ends when
you finally do

2.

Every time you roll your
eyes
an angel gets the axe

3.

I don't have a favorite
chair anymore
She'll say
I don't enjoy complexity
like I think I might have
You'll say
Here is a better life loved
through confusion
You'll both agree
Let the Dead Bury the Dead
Said a movie
It's complicated
The Universe whispers
Don't ask

SOIREE

Across a crowded room
he motioned to her
in broken semaphore
¿How do you feel?
and luckily she had written
a 900 page book
the night before
explaining why
she couldn't explain
how she felt and
so she mailed it to him
packaged with some
crudités from a sad
platter on her side
of the room
and when it arrived
on his side
the party was over
the guests having shrugged
themselves to indifference
and disappeared in a
haze of ennui and
disappointed sex
leaving them a vast

and empty space
they could finally wander
across as lonely nomads
and find each other –
read her book together
and agree that the weather
inside them was the same

HERE

She said
I thought you might
like to fall off this –
and she presented
a block of marble
tall enough
to mean something
if he fell from it after
he chiseled out
a likeness of her
but his hands were
too heavy as it was
his heart an anchor
her face
something to buoy
his dread – get it
off the floor of the sea
turn it into something
to raise a glass to
at any gathering
of doubters
Here's to Love
He would say
and mean it

like a sculptor
finishing her likeness
to perfection
by never starting it
in the 1st place

THE GREAT JIU JITSU MOVE OF BEING

Stand like a horse
on a street named
Your Grandmother's Best Friend Who Made You
Grilled Cheese Used To Live Here Rd.
and with your back
to the sun
name just one person
who would die for you
or melt cheese for you
next realize
you should have spent a lifetime
learning to sing for her
or ringing the neck
of a trombone for her
or how to move like water
so she can float down you
– A. River
nothing roiling
just a ride for her
all her shitty memories vague
and quiet now

THE CONCERT

¡Look
She said
I brought you an orchestra!
And she unveiled a cello
crawling with golden
termites
Actually
He said
You brought me
the end of the world –
The end of the world
She replied
Would have been
a saxophone tarnished
with your suspicion
and doubt my dear –
he agreed that would
have been a hopeless
concert no one
would attend
and so they settled into
the comfort that was
uniquely theirs
and moved to the sound
of the world turning to dust

DIE A LITTLE MORE

A kiss in a 1967 Alfa Romeo
equals a movie his father
would never have recommended
but
it happened anyway
only without the words
Il mio [quare] cuore!
that she would have breathed
in that movie if:
A. She spoke Italian
and
B. They weren't in her mother's Datsun
that story ends in a novel
about time travel left un-
read on a table on the set of a play
starring Marcello Mastroianni
in a white lab coat
smoking a cigarette
being unintelligible but cool
and she explained it to him
like a goddess gifting him
a 20 minute fever-memory
ending in red

HAMMERS

¿Why do you carry
that thing around?
He asked
Same reason you do
She said
and they looked down
at the precious
delicate thing
on the pedestal
between them –
brought their eyes
up to each other
– he
looking for clues
– she
arranging the furniture
in her head for a place
to fall elegantly and
tightening
the grip
on her handle

INFINITY WAR

Standing
arms crossed
like a newly minted god
He told her
I love you
Me too
She said
Well I love you
times infinity
He said this time
with a little more starch
in his backbone –
and looking up from
from some tiny
intricate thing
she was always doing
with her hands
when he came to her
She said
It's not a competition
and he saw now that
she had been carving
out of some
as yet undiscovered stuff
a miniature world

for them to inhabit someday
– It kind of is
He shook from his
closing throat

THE ART OF THINKING ON EARTH AT 3:13 AM

It'll only bother you
if you think about it –
She had told him
when asked about the
dinner she would be
eating on Mars with
the previous owner
of her iron heart –
now – with her enjoying
0.375 gravity
and him without a
spaceship
he let his mind wander
a museum of possibilities
until he found himself
in its unlit cellar
– at night
with an unseen hand
guiding him in circles
like a clueless lion arcing
around a hunter who
at this distance
couldn't miss

THE IMPOSSIBILITY OF SOME SITUATIONS

When she (finally) came home
She found him in a chair surrounded
by 12 small elephants

¿What's with the elephants
She asked like a prison guard
who had just discovered a hatchet
under an inmate's bunk

I had a dream while you
were away
He explained
I missed you
so you sent me 12 elephants
to keep me company
until you came back
In the dream you told me
they were the animals most
capable of sympathizing
with loneliness and longing

I would never send elephants
to anyone like that
She said

I know
He said

But
when I woke up from the dream
they were all here and
now they won't leave me

They can't stay here
She said

I know
He said
But they won't leave

Well
She said
It's them or me

He looked down at the smallest elephant he had taken
to be their leader and waited for a sign

It came in the form of a wink
timed
to the sound of a closing door

And he was astonished to find

(Because he was sure
he had seen all
the documentaries
about elephants)

That they could
smile

WAKING TO THE SOUND OF CRACKING

He pulled a ghost
from himself
after dreaming her –
his head like an empty
theater suddenly full of
doubt and inconvenient
sensibilities and no
audience to laugh him
back to his senses –
only the indifference of
another unwelcome
morning – the sun lagging
behind – now he thought
he should have a surgeon
on retainer to mend
that thawing place
where she lay like
summer on him
his winter returning
when she left
his sleep
a story he kept
forgetting not
to trust

HOW TO LOVE A GHOST

Don't take that blank
stare personally –
she's off somewhere
less stifling than here
and your touch
was a nice try
but she can't feel it and
reciprocation would be
like breaking a promise
she never made to
someone she haunted
and left languishing
in a waiting room
in Duluth four
presidents ago
so just sleep it off
and when you wake
don't look for her
she's off counting
all the letters from all
the waiting rooms
holding the haunted more
alive than you'll ever be
and kept in boxes marked
"Maybe Someday"

BOREDOM WASTED ON THE BORED

When they locked eyes
and wished for some
peace and quiet
they didn't mean for
the car to crash into
the telephone pole
a mile away and kill
the power –
but that's what happened
so they did the logical
things –
he picked up
a pen
and she
a knife
– 41 minutes later
the fish tank
started gurgling
again and lights woke
dropping their shadows
across the drop cloth
they put down to scribble
and carve themselves
a place in the world

where she'd hold him down
at the point of a stiletto
with one hand
and feed him
cilantro with
the other

IT'S NOT LOVE TILL SOMEONE LOSES AN EYE

I should warn you
She said
Two of my former lovers
were dragged to their
deaths by wild horses

¿Only two?
He asked

Yes
She said tightening
her legs around him
But the horses part was
metaphorical

and he noticed the
sun had rolled off
to somewhere
it could be more
useful

BREAKFAST ALL DAY

He explained to God that he had just had
the best breakfast in the best place ever
That diner
God said
Is just a cemetery with a pond
in the middle to drown in
they fish the bodies out and bury them
in the surrounding hills
I know
He said
Also
Continued God
To get here
you climbed into a car
full of men with scarred faces
I know
He said
And all the water
God said
The leaking roof
and it wasn't even raining
I know
He said
But the omelet was perfect

The omelet was a little dry
God said
But the music was perfect
He said
There was none
God said
She spoke and
He said
that was music
She stared and the rain stopped
She fed me from her fork so the food *was* delicious
and those surrounding hills moved beyond the horizon
He remembered
This conversation is boring
He said
because – my God
you weren't there

REGNUM DEFENDE

Imagine –
There's a song playing
so good it deserves
its own playlist
and the parking is like
a confusion of dories
at the end of a whale
slaughter and you're running
up stairs dodging tumbling
household appliances thrown
by the god of mini-fridges
and you're trying like hell
and a wheezing Neruda
to warn her before
that morning star
catches you
but you can only
manage inch-long
words exhaled like
regrets you didn't know
you had till now
and whispered
in the wrong ear
but this is a dream

– you think
or at least a perfect
movie about Bond
James
that is
and the moral is simple –
it's possible to hold
a monarchy in contempt
and still love a queen

OF A FEATHER

Don't come near me
She said from the
other side of the door
I smell like a dumpster
I have no joy in me
And I'm tired
so he walked for 1000 miles
and presented his sad
dusty shoes to her and asked
¿This tired?
Yes – She said
he screwed
Rachmaninoff into
his ears for hours
presented himself
weeping in D minor 7th
to her and said
¿This sad?
Yes – She said
he put his broken
heart on a platter
of food and threw it
into a dumpster
behind a 5-star restaurant

then rummaged around
for days to retrieve it
¿This smelly?
He asked
Yes – She said
and she invited him inside
to sit with her among
shards of ostraca
handed him some glue
rearranged the pieces
to make a place
to nest – and after counting
and laughing about
everyone they loved who
wasn't lucky enough to be them –
  Slept

I DREAMED YOU DAMMIT

She said
and he looked at the hole
in the ground where she
had spun on her heel

and he thought maybe
he'd killed someone
in her head – counted
like Berryman all
the persons he knew
– they were all still there
in this world

but in her head
there might be blood

he remembered
her claim
that he had massacred
her on canvas

she had taken a flight
to somewhere so
she could break that news

by telegram
from as far away as
possible

so maybe
– just maybe

THE ARRIVALIST

That's the worst song
I've ever heard
She said
Actually
She continued
It's worse than just
the worst – It's like
the goddesses
of bad music had an orgy
and they all came at the
same time and made
that song appear – ¿where
did you find it?
I wrote it for you this morning
He answered
and he started to explain
that he hadn't been feeling
quite himself – that maybe
he'd suffered a stroke – etc
she silenced him with a finger
to his lips – leaned in and said
I love it like my life

– and she meant it

THE PROBLEMS SHOW

There's only one path to God
she said
I think I know what you mean
¿Buffalo, New York right?
He said
No
She said
You have to stand naked
on the roof of an empty
parking garage and
check your wallet
like
really check it
(she made wonderful emphasizing noises)
¿If I'm naked
how do I check my wallet?
He asked
Where is it kept?
You know like when
you hear a piano
trilling some lounge music
behind a closed and locked door
in a building with no windows
She said

And you just know someone's getting
strangled on the other side?
No
He said
I'm not a lounge-y person
He said
Well
there
in that feeling
folded and pressed into
your wallet
She said
You'll find the currency to
buy an audience with the Almighty
then
as if to put a finer point on it
she exploded into brilliance and light like
in the movies only
he was the only audience for this
effervescent punctuation
there was smoke too
and when the smoke cleared
he found he was in the pocket of God
with all the spare change of the world

METAMORPHOSIS

He glanced over at her
and saw an emu where
she was just sitting
¿Why are you an emu now?
He asked
I thought you liked emus
She answered
You said so the other day
I did
He said
But I like *you* better
You didn't add that part
She came back
I didn't think I had to
He wanted to say but
by now his throat
was closing
like a border crossing
between his thoughts
and her tears just
now welling up
¿So now that I'm an emu
you love me less?
She said the words
as if pruning dead leaves

from a hopeless plant
¿Is it reversible?
He asked
No
She said
Good!
He smiled
I can hold up a book
so you can read to me
I see you have no arms
I'd love that
She said
and closing his eyes
he still marveled at the sound
of her voice

SLEEP

That is – a sleep
sketchy at best but
that gave him time
to dream trees
turned to lumber
to build the perfect
chair for her to sit
on and tell him
her story (and it
was a good story)
about needing
a better arborist
to grow better trees
for a better carpenter
to build a better chair
for lounging and talking
about wants vs needs
 – or that's what he heard
as he listened like
a doctor searching
for the last word
in someone's head
finding only his
#bigdumbmistake

of waiting too long
to tell her about the ache
she planted in his chest
for her hands – her smile
or his impatience for
her body arching like
a bridge from the tip
of his tongue to her
halting breath
and how he was a ship
wrecked on the rocks
every time she left
taking all his skills
of navigation with her
– leaving him alone
to work on building
a chair she may never sit on

WHEN SCIENCE TOOK OVER
OR
HOW TO BELIEVE A QUEEN WHEN SHE SAYS "I LOVE YOU"

He built a contraption
to trap a queen's thoughts
– a gimbaled thing
so he could examine them
upright – even on the rough
sea of his doubt – and in her
forlorn face and sleepstarved eyes
where even gravity didn't
stand a chance
he died
over and over
A king believes no one –
He thought – but
A *good* king will spend
a lifetime believing a queen
who asked only the kingdom
of his body to rest on
and sleep

ON A SELF-DRIVING COUCH TO SOMEWHERE

They held each other
so close the sun skipped
out of town to give them
some privacy – afterwards
they entered the kingdom
of overused words – "Love"
was on a pedestal with
a sign reading "Find a
Synonym for This One
and Stay Away From it"
they cried at this like
gardeners with empty
watering cans during
a drought and they used
the word on each other
so successfully
so correctly – finally
giving the word it's due
like no one before them
– exchanging smiles they
paid the toll to get out
of that place
and never
looked
back

EPILOGUE

THE GODLESS NIGHT KITCHEN (REMODELED)

Where day is overcooked
and blackened to night
and the wind comes drumming
a memory of the yesterday's
morning
while everyone else is sleeping
more soundly than him and
his nimble fingers awake
at the abacus

He finds he and she add up
to something like unwelcome
religion
over and over again

And smiles are contraband
to each other
and in the morning he'll wake
before her when
someone comes to him and
tells the truth of what
an unfinished symphony
they are

And that all hearts are designed
to harden and crack.

There are birds in there

That's how they get out

ACKNOWLEDGMENTS

"The Ungulate" appeared in *Jubilat*.

ABOUT THE AUTHOR

Clay Ventre lives and writes in New England.

42° 19' 47.9" N 70° 56' 43.9" W

Nixes Mate is a navigational hazard in Boston Harbor used during the colonial period to gibbet and hang pirates and mutineers.

Nixes Mate Books features small-batch artisanal literature, created by writers who use all 26 letters of the alphabet and then some, honing their craft the time-honored way: one line at a time.

nixesmate.pub

www.ingramcontent.com/pod-product-compliance
Lightning Source LLC
Chambersburg PA
CBHW051808100526
44592CB00016B/2621